Published in the UK in 1994 by
Schofield & Sims Limited, Huddersfield, England.

0 7217 5011 7

Foods

Schofield & Sims Limited Huddersfield.

Milk

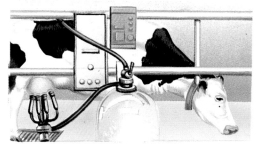

Cows are milked twice a day, mostly by machine. The milk flows through tubes into a container.

The milk is then pumped into a tank where it is cooled. A tanker transports the milk to a dairy.

The milk that we drink is usually cow's milk. Milk is rich in the vitamins and *calcium* that our bodies need in order to grow properly.

At the dairy, milk is heated in order to kill any *germs*. This is called pasteurisation. The milk is then cooled and put into bottles.

Milk comes in many different forms. There is fresh milk, powdered milk, skimmed milk, and condensed milk (which sometimes comes in a tube!).

Cheese

If milk is exposed to air for a few hours, it changes its appearance and its taste. It becomes curdled. People have invented all kinds of ways of using curdled milk to make cheese. The first cheese was probably made over 4000 years ago.

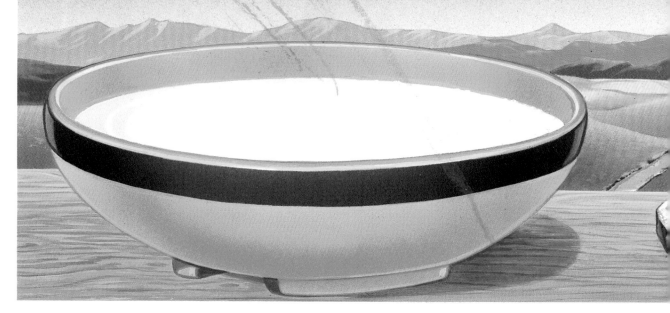

Cheese can be made from the milk of cows, sheep or goats.

Cheeses come in many different shapes and sizes. Some cheeses are hard and have holes in them. Others are soft and round, with a thick white rind.

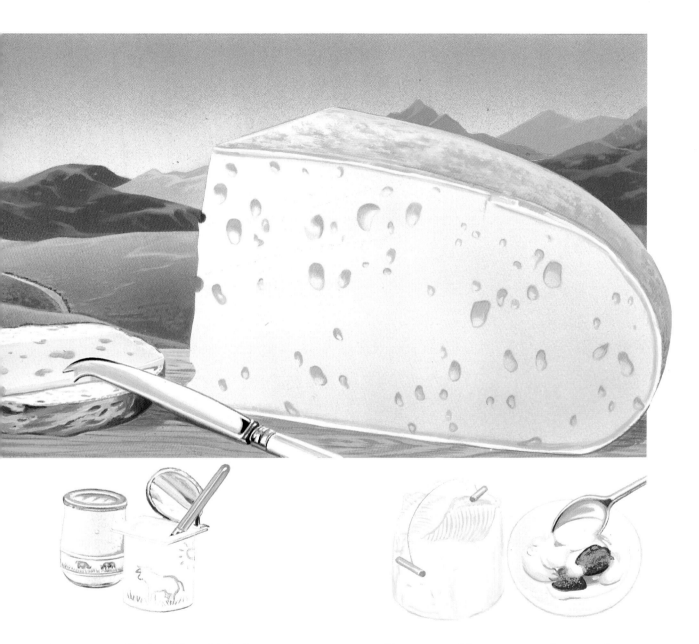

Yoghurt is curdled milk which has been gently heated. It often has fruit or flavouring added.

Cream and butter are also made from milk. Butter is made by beating cream.

Bread

The grains are then transported
to the flour mill, where machines
crush them to make flour.

At the bakery, a little water, salt
and yeast are mixed with the
flour to make a dough.

To make bread, we need flour. Flour is made from many different cereals such as barley, rye or oats, and, of course, wheat. When the wheat is ripe, it is cut and collected by a combine harvester.

Next, the baker shapes the dough into lumps to make bread. Later, these will be put into the oven to bake.

Flour is used throughout the world to make all kinds of bread, in many different shapes and flavours.

Sugar

Sugar gives us energy faster than any other food.

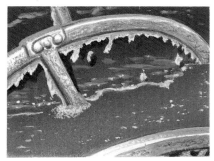

Sugar-cane is usually cut by hand. The stems are transported to a mill, where they are washed and shredded. The shredded stems are then crushed to obtain the sweet juice.

The root of the sugar-beet contains sugar. The leafy green tops are cut off and fed to cattle. A machine digs up the roots, which are then crushed to extract the juice.

Sugar is obtained from certain plants such as sugar-cane and sugar-beet.

The sugar we eat can be white, brown, *crystallised*, in powder form, or in cubes. Sugar is white when it is *refined*. Raw sugar is yellowish-brown in colour.

Sugar is used to make all kinds of sweets, as well as cakes and pastries. Although sugar gives us energy, dentists say that too much sugar is bad for our teeth and causes decay.

Salt

Sea salt is harvested from salt-marshes. Sea water is stored in shallow ponds called salt-pans. There, it *evaporates* through the action of the sun and the wind.

The salt that is collected in this way forms into large crystals, which are then cleaned and dried.

The salt used in food comes mainly from the sea. Salt is important for our health. That is why salt was once considered to be as valuable as gold. Today, people are advised not to eat too much salt.

Long ago, salt was used to *preserve* foods such as ham, fish and beef.

There is also a lot of salt in underground mines. This type of salt is called rock salt.

Oil

Oil is a food that contains many elements, such as vitamins, which are needed for growth. Oil is made from the seed, the nut or the fruit of different plants, such as rapeseed, groundnut, sunflower or maize.

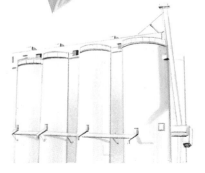

After harvesting, the grains or seeds are stored in huge silos before being despatched to a *refinery*.

Oil is also obtained from the fruit of a tropical tree, the palm nut. The *kernel* of the nut contains almond oil and the *pulp* yields palm oil.

Olive trees grow in hot, sunny lands. The olives are picked, washed and then pressed. The oil which is obtained will be *refined* before being bottled and sold.

Some animals and fish also provide oil. Cod-liver oil, for example, is very good for you.

13

Chocolate

The beans are dried in the sun and turn dark red in colour. They are then despatched to a factory.

The roasted and crushed beans are made into cocoa paste. Grease from this is extracted and used in beauty products.

Chocolate is made from the fruit of the cacao tree, which grows in hot and humid regions. The flowers produce large fruits, called pods, which are yellowish-orange in colour. The pods are split in two to remove the white beans.

The remainder of the paste is turned into a powder. This cocoa powder is used to make drinking chocolate.

The dark, or plain, chocolate that we eat is made from pure cocoa. Milk and sugar are added to this to make it into milk chocolate.

15

Coffee

Coffee comes from the berries of the coffee plant. The berries are harvested when they are mature and firm and bright red in colour. They are usually picked by hand. Sometimes, the plant is shaken to make the berries fall off.

Next, the berries are washed and then left to dry for several days. They are turned over regularly, using large rakes. When the berries are dry, they are shelled to extract the coffee beans inside.

The beans are packed into strong sacks so that they can be transported more easily.

The coffee beans are blended and roasted to make different flavours, before being put into packets or boxes.

Coffee can be sold in many forms – beans, granules, grounds or powder. You can drink it with or without milk, cream or sugar.

Cereals

These ears of maize, or corn-cobs, can be eaten as a vegetable or made into cornflour or semolina. The corn *kernels* can also be made into the puffs or flakes that we see in our breakfast cereals.

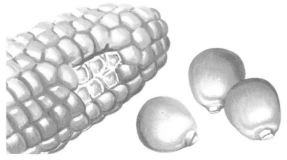

When the maize crop is ripe, the cobs are harvested and the *kernels* are picked off them. Sugar, salt and malt are added to them before they are cooked or baked.

When the *kernels* are cooked, they can be crushed to make cornflakes or they can be kept whole to make popcorn.

The different corn products are then put into packets to be sold in the shops.

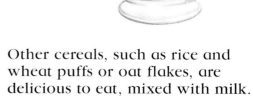

Other cereals, such as rice and wheat puffs or oat flakes, are delicious to eat, mixed with milk.

Wine

Grapes are harvested at the beginning of autumn. This is called the vintage. The bunches of grapes are either cut by hand, using secateurs, or by machine.

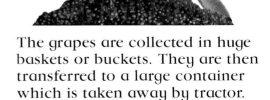

The grapes are collected in huge baskets or buckets. They are then transferred to a large container which is taken away by tractor.

The fruit of the vine plant, the red or white grape, can be eaten or can be made into alcoholic drinks – white, rosé or red wine.

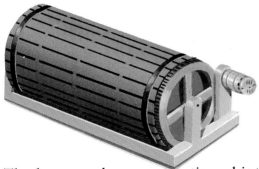

The harvested grapes are tipped into a wine-press which crushes the grapes. Next, the grape juice is put into a large cask where *fermentation* takes place.

The wine is now put into casks to develop its flavour. Later, it will be filtered and bottled. Some wine is stored in casks for years.

The Potato

The potato came originally from South America. Today, it is one of the world's main food crops and is grown in many countries. Potatoes were introduced into Europe during the 16th century.

In autumn, huge machines are used to dig up the potato crop.

There are very many different kinds of potato. The new potato has a thin skin and does not keep for very long. It needs to be eaten as soon as possible.

Potatoes can be eaten mashed, boiled,
roasted, baked, fried, or as chips. The *starch*
from potatoes is used in making cakes.

Honey

Honey is made by honey-bees. The taste and smell of honey can vary, depending on whether the pollen has come from the acacia tree, or from lavender or clover plants, for example.

When honey needs to be collected, the beekeeper uses smoke to disperse the bees before removing the roof of the hive.

The beekeeper then lifts out the honeycombs and uses a knife to scrape off the wax caps which cover the honey-filled *alveoli*.

Next, the honeycombs are put into a machine to allow the honey in the *alveoli* to run out.

Honey is used to make sweets, cakes and pastries. Or you can simply spread it on a slice of bread.

Glossary

Alveoli
The cells in a honeycomb where the bees store their honey.

Calcium
An element that is necessary for growth because it strengthens bones and teeth. It is found in milk and other dairy products.

Crystallise
To form into a clear, solid shape.

Evaporate
When water is heated by the sun, it is turned into tiny droplets which float in the air. We say the water has evaporated.

Fermentation
Breaking down a substance by the action of yeast or bacteria.

Germs
Tiny organisms which often cause illness.

Kernel
The whole seed of a nut or cereal.

Preserve
To keep food in good condition, it can be preserved in different ways – by keeping it cool or by salting it, for example.

Pulp
The soft flesh of vegetables and fruit.

Refine
To make something more pure.

Starch
A floury substance obtained mainly from potatoes or cereals.